THE GREAT WALL

THE GENIUS OF CHINA · A CLOSE-UP GUIDE

THE GREAT WALL

What makes it "Great"?

Each day an astonishing 10,000 tourists, Chinese and foreign, travel 65 kilometres north of Beijing to visit Badaling, the section of the Great Wall nearest to the capital. These large numbers of visitors look like ants swarming on its mighty ramparts. As they look west, their eyes follow the stone dragon dipping and thrusting to the horizon. Imagination takes them beyond, towards the vast interior of China, where 2,500 kilometres away, the Great Wall has its distant beginning. In the opposite direction the ramparts roll east, to the coast of the Bohai Sea, 450 kilometres away.

Built to defend the Middle Kingdom from the barbarians of Central Asia and Mongolia, the Great Wall is undaunted by any landscape on its course, from the remote fortress of Jiayuguan in Gansu Province to its seaside terminus at Old Dragon's Head in Shanhaiguan. But little of the Great Wall is like that at Badaling. A serpent of mud in the Gobi tracts of Gansu, it skirts and has been half buried by the advancing dunes of the Tengger and Ordos Deserts. Only after crossing the Yellow River for the second time, on its journey from desert to sea, does the Great Wall become stone-blocked, in Hebei Province's Yanshan Mountains, to the north and east of Beijing.

At 2,950 kilometres, it is a *long* wall. But perhaps the fact that truly makes the Great Wall so remarkable is that it represents ancient mankind's most enduring intrusion on any landscape. For the Great Wall is of a scale so mighty and imposing that it dominates whatever desert, valley and mountain it traverses. Over the centuries it has become part of the geography of northern China, familiar to generations of peasants who have lived in its shadow.

It is a Wonder of the World, perhaps *the* Wonder. Decades would be required to inspect all its remaining sections. The Great Wall is not a single structure, but rather the result of previously existing walls, linked and extended. Constructed over some 1,835 years, from the Qin Dynasty (221-206 BC) to the Ming Dynasty (1368-1644), it tells us a great deal about China's civilization, her legends, innovations, and indeed the xenophobic mind which forced

(Preceding page) Invaders' view of the Wall — formidable. (Top) Brickwork of a watchtower. (Bottom) Most of the remains of the Great Wall date from the massive reconstruction undertaken during the Ming Dynasty . This Wall, marking the present-day border between Shanxi and Inner Mongolia, was built during the reign of Zhengtong in the mid-15th century.

(Top) Loophole for cannon or archers. (Bottom) Shandan County in Gansu's Hexi Corridor boasts the best-preserved rammed earth sections of the Ming Great Wall, totalling some 90 kilometres in length. (Following page) Distant beginning — the very western end of the Ming Dynasty Great Wall on a cliff above the Taolai River near Jiayuguan, Gansu Province. (Pages 6-7) Little of the Great Wall is like the section at Badaling. Watchtowers and the ramparts were made from rammed earth for most of its length. (Inset) The Wall streaks along the foot of the Wushao Hills, east of Wuwei, Gansu.

the countless millions of labourers into working on the largest defensive project in human history.

Travellers have always been awe-struck by their first sight of the Great Wall. Lord Macartney, an envoy of Britain's George III, passed through the mighty defences at Gubeikou in 1793, *en route* to Jehol (now Chengde) on a mission to open up trade with Emperor Qianlong (reigned 1736-95). A member of his entourage calculated that the volume of building material in the Chinese structure exceeded that in all the buildings in the United Kingdom of the day. Mildred Cable, an English missionary, approached the western terminus at Jiayuguan in the 1930s by horse and cart. She wrote in her travelogue, *The Gobi Desert*, that the "absurd structure" continued "irrespective of difficulties until it reached the sea, 1,400 miles away." A French traveller, Comte de Beauvoir, was more poetic, writing that the Wall "would be stored in my mind like a magic vision forever."

But US President Richard Nixon, walking on the Wall at Badaling in 1972, summed up in a few simple words what many had taken hundreds to say: "Yes, it really is a *great* wall."

Origins and Evolution — who masterminded the Great Wall and which emperors inherited the Wall-building mania?

There were several walls, great in terms of the distances they stretched, before the Great Wall. But, in a fundamental sense, none of them was the Great Wall of China. That is because they were built before China, as an empire, existed. During the Warring States period (475-221 BC), the eastern and central part of what is now China was divided into as many as 12 regional kingdoms. They were in a constant state of war, hence many cities of the time were protected by walls.

Wall-building entered a new era when the casting of iron allowed

(Top) A Hui nationality (Moslem) shepherd grazes his flock around a derelict fortress on the Great Wall in Ningxia. (Bottom) This Wall at Jiayuguan shows the ledge along which guards would have walked between watchtowers. (Following page) The snaking Wall at Shabukou, north of Datong, marks the present-day border between Shanxi and Inner Mongolia. (Pages 10-11) Midwinter panorama over the Wall zigzagging toward the distant and perilous Jinshanling Ridge.

arsenals of various fearsome weapons to be made. This offensive threat resulted in defensive moves to match. Iron tools made the construction of long walls across open country a feasibility from around the early 4th century BC. The first long-distance walls were constructed on the borders of the warring kingdoms, mainly of rammed earth, but sometimes of stone, by whichever state was content to define its limit of conquest. Only traces of these inter-kingdom walls remain today.

Apart from the walls between kingdoms, the Yan, Zhao and Qin states of the north built walls to defend themselves against the nomads of the steppes. Around that time the Kingdom of Qin began to conquer neighbouring states and, under Ying Zheng in 221 BC, *Zhongguo*, the Middle Kingdom, came into being. Ying Zheng called himself Qin Shihuangdi—the First Emperor of the Qin Dynasty. And from the word Qin

(pronounced *chin*) the name of China is derived.

Qin Shihuangdi became the first emperor of China. Inter-kingdom walls, built during the Warring States period, were demolished, but those in the north still served a purpose—to act as a division between the civilized empire of China and the barbarian nomads. Qin Shihuangdi entrusted one of his generals, Meng Tian, with the task of using the existing walls of Yan, Zhao and part of the former Qin kingdom defence as a framework on which to build the first Great Wall (221-210 BC). Remnants of this Qin Great Wall still exist in the vicinity of Lintao, south of Gansu Province's capital, Lanzhou.

Qin Shihuangdi died in 210 BC and was buried in an elaborate mausoleum near Xi'an, "protected"

by thousands of life-sized terracotta warriors.

Just four years after his death, the Qin Dynasty was overthrown by Liu Bang, who founded the Han Dynasty in 206 BC. Over the next 1,819 years many emperors would continue the idea of Wall-building. Some renovated, strengthened or extended the Great Wall they inherited. Others built ramparts in new locations to consolidate their territorial conquests. Some abandoned Wall-building altogether.

Han rulers extended the empire, particularly towards Central Asia. The Hexi Corridor, just north of the Qilian Mountains and south of the Badain Jaran Desert, was a natural route to the heart of the continent. Merchants began forging a route that eventually became known as the Silk Road. However, the Xiongnu tribe frequently attacked those travelling along it. To protect caravans on the route, the Great Wall was extended from Lintao, the western terminus of the Qin Great Wall, westwards through the Hexi Corridor to Yumenguan. Watchtowers were built between Yumenguan, the "Jade Gate", and Dunhuang. The Han extension of the Great Wall was also a spur to colonize recently conquered lands. Garrisons were stationed along the Wall in newly-established prefectures, such as Wuwei, Zhangye and Jiuquan in Gansu Province.

After the fall of the Han Dynasty in 220 AD, the empire disintegrated into conflict that lasted almost two centuries. Then came 250 years of Wall-building, first by the Wei, Zhou and Qi Dynasties (collectively known as the Northern Dynasties, 386-581 AD) and then, after the empire was re-unified, by the Sui Dynasty (581-618), particularly under the rule of Yangdi. He is said to have utilized a million men to build an earthwork south of the Yellow River's big loop in a period of one week. Yangdi also initiated China's second greatest mass-labour project, the Grand Canal.

(Preceding page) Principal gate on the Wall in Shanhaiguan called "The First Pass Under Heaven". (Top) The standard design for watchtowers was put forward by General Qi Jiguang of the Ming Dynasty. The structures protrude by several metres on the north side, allowing archers in the tower to shoot from the flank at invaders scaling the Wall. (Bottom) Dawn over Mutianyu, a tourist section of Wall north of Beijing.

Centuries ensued when the Great Wall was a redundant defence. During the Tang Dynasty (618-907), the empire was pushed well beyond the boundary of the Great Wall. Moreover, the period was characterized by international exchange rather than the xenophobia and isolationism that Wall-building represented.

It was not until the establishment of the Jin Dynasty (1115-1234), of northeastern origin, that Wall-building recommenced. Ramparts were built across what is today Inner Mongolia, Jilin, Heilongjiang and the People's

(Top) The Jiayuguan fortress is located against the backdrop of the Qilian Mountains. (Bottom) A formidable defence as seen from the land of barbarians. (Following page) A midsummer's panorama over Badaling.

Republic of Mongolia. Few traces of the structure remain, since the region is swept by sand-laden storms and heavy snows.

The beginning of the final and most spectacular chapter in the 1,835–year history of the Great Wall's construction was the Mongol invasion of 1211. The Chinese suffered under Yuan Dynasty rule until 1368. Liberation from this dark age came with an Anhui peasant, Zhu Yuanzhang, who led armies to oust the Mongols. He established a dynasty called Ming, which means bright, and took the reign name Hongwu.

Paranoid that invasion would again lead to foreign rule, the early Ming emperors, beginning with Hongwu, started a systematic reconstruction of the Great Wall. Hongwu's successor but one, Yongle (1403-1424), built much of the Great Wall to the north of Beijing. Xuande (1426-1436) continued his work in Hebei, while his alleged son, Zhengtong/Tianshun (1436-1450, 1457-1464), was responsible for the "belt and braces" strategy of a second line of defence—the Interior Great Wall, of which Juyongguan is a part. Construction also took place westward, across Shanxi, Shaanxi and into Gansu. This extensive work continued during the rule of Chenghua (1465-1486). All this construction was on an unprecedented scale, accomplished with millions of labourers working at any one time.

The Ming emperors of the late 16th century channelled their efforts into adding more watchtowers along the section to the east of the Yellow River. The last part of the construction, an eastward extension known as the Liaodong Sidewall, is thought to have taken place around 1614, during the reign of Wanli (1573-1620). Ramparts were built from eastern

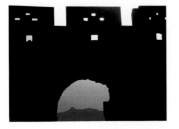

(Preceding pages) Towers inside the Jiayuguan fortress, western end of Great Wall. (Inset) Kazak nationality descendant of nomadic tribes on the Silk Road. (Top) Mighty and imposing, the Great Wall has become part of the geography of north China. (Bottom) A silhouetted watchtower at Simatai, Luanping County, shows the embrasures in the battlements on the upper storey.

Liaoning Province to the estuary of the Yalu River.

Despite the efforts made by the Ming emperors to build what was the strongest Great Wall in the long history of its construction, it was defensively only as strong as its weakest link. That proved to be at Shanhaiguan on the Bohai coast, where tens of thousands of Manchu horsemen streamed through the narrow pass between mountain and sea in 1644, to establish the Qing Dynasty (1644-1911).

Nevertheless, the legacy of the Ming is a seemingly indestructible monument to more than 18 centuries of man's mind and muscle, a stark reminder of his ingenuity and barbarity, as permanent an epitaph as there could be to the millions of labourers who built it.

Mind and Muscle—the design and construction of the ramparts

The steep-sided valley at Juyongguan, a strategic pass on the Interior Great Wall to the north of Beijing, has been a hive of building activity since the beginning of the 1990s. The ramparts, originally built around 1440 during the reign of Zhengtong, were dismantled by locals in search of building materials during the Qing Dynasty and the Republican period (1911-1949). In 1995, these ramparts were reconstructed to provide a further section of the Wall for the growing number of tourists. Throughout that summer, scenes of Wall-building, by methods virtually unchanged since Ming Dynasty times, could be seen and heard—the hammering and chiselling of rock; the sawing of whole tree trunks; the loading of mules with bricks, blocks, timber and mortar. Under the crack of the muleteers' whips, overloaded animals climbed 320 metres above the valley floor on narrow, zigzagging paths, to deliver the materials to work gangs. Men dug trenches with shovels and moved boulders with their bare hands. Blocks of granite, quarried locally, were chiselled to fit together perfectly. The only mechanization was rudimentary—block and tackle, used to heave up timbers in the construction of a watchtower.

(Top) Pavements are flat on level or gently sloping sections. (Bottom) This watchtower can be seen to have a block base topped with bricks and is positioned on a peak where the Wall changes direction.

Primitive as these methods might appear, there is no other way of building a wall on slopes as steep as 60 degrees from horizontal. This terrain is only accessible on foot or horseback.

The routing of the Great Wall along the high mountain ridges and across steep slopes was a fundamental policy of the architects and engineers of the ramparts. Their main consideration was entirely military—defence of the empire and the swift communication of warnings in the event of invasion. Building on the high, rugged terrain not only accentuated the defensive capacity of the Wall, but saved on building materials and provided guards manning the Wall with a clear vantage point from which to survey the surrounding countryside. Moreover, the Great Wall was made to appear insurmountable to any invader.

Construction across rugged mountain terrain was physically demanding for the labour force, but with an almost infinite supply of workers, this was of no consideration to the ministers of war, under whose jurisdiction the Great Wall fell.

They instructed the governors of military garrisons to build the Wall or "recruited" masses of labourers specifically for the purpose. For example, four prefectural governors—of Wuwei, Zhangye, Jiuquan and Dunhuang—were put in charge of the construction through Gansu, in the time of Emperor Wudi during the Han Dynasty. In Ming Dynasty times, the whole section of Wall between Jiayuguan and Shanhaiguan was divided into nine *zhen* (military regions). Inevitably, individual commanders won recognition for vigorous construction successes. General Huo Qubing won favour with Wudi for building the Great Wall in Jiuquan, while in Ming times General Qi Jiguang received imperial praise for watchtower construction

between Beijing and Shanhaiguan.

Using locally available materials—earth, stone, timber and reed—was a practice adhered to throughout Wall-building history. Stone was quarried locally to build the ramparts in mountainous areas. On flatter terrain, earth was moistened and rammed with poles and hammers between bamboo frames, and finally this baked hard in the sun. In desert areas, where the sand had no adhesion even when moistened, ramparts were built of alternating layers of sand and tamarisk twigs or reeds.

Wall-building made strides when bricks, tiles and mortar began to be used during the Ming Dynasty. They were baked in kilns located as close to the construction work as possible. Markings on some bricks tell the location and date of their manufacture.

Despite the availability of materials locally, some transport by man, sometimes using tools or animals, was often necessary. Labourers usually stood in long lines to pass blocks and bricks up the mountain. Some used bamboo poles on their shoulders or had materials strapped to their backs. Simple tools were employed to shift heavier blocks and timbers. They included levers, wheelbarrows, ropes and winches. Draught animals, particularly mules and goats, were used in mountain areas, while camels were preferred in the west.

The ramparts of the Ming Dynasty Great Wall in the mountains were built in fairly similar styles, depending on the strategic importance of the area. Defences are trapezoidal or oblong in cross-section, with the inside and outside walls seven to eight metres in height. They are composed of large stone-block bases, topped with bricks. These rest on foundations seven to eight metres in breadth, that go up to one and a half metres deep into the mountainside.

On the more gentle slopes (less than 45 degrees) the blocks and bricks above ground run parallel to the slope. On steeper terrain, the blocks and bricks were laid in a stepped fashion. Blocks, most commonly of granite or other igneous rocks, were large and weighty. Therefore, they did not require any mortar to bind

(Preceding page) As a measure of extra security," mini battlements" were constructed on short sections of the Wall as pictured here, in Luanping County. They would have allowed guards to fight invaders who had successfully scaled the ramparts. (Top) Brilliant dawn sunlight pierces the dark chambers of a watchtower at Jinshanling. (Bottom) Watchtowers were built within arrow-shot, thus making the structure actively defended along its entire length.

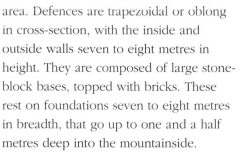

(Bottom) Block and tackle was the only mechanical aid used in recent reconstruction at Juyongguan, here in the building of a watchtower. (Far right top) High above the valley at Juyongguan, Wall renovation in the mid-1990s was still labour-intensive.

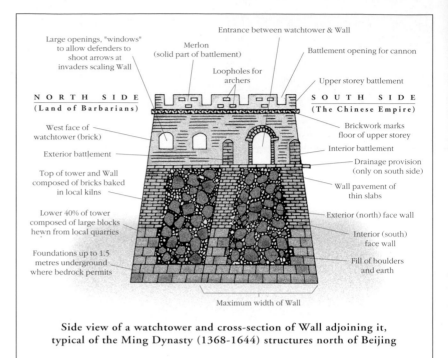

Large openings, "windows" to allow defenders to shoot arrows at invaders scaling Wall

Merlon (solid part of battlement)

Entrance between watchtower & Wall

Battlement opening for cannon

Loopholes for archers

Upper storey battlement

NORTH SIDE (Land of Barbarians)

SOUTH SIDE (The Chinese Empire)

West face of watchtower (brick)

Brickwork marks floor of upper storey

Exterior battlement

Interior battlement

Top of tower and Wall composed of bricks baked in local kilns

Drainage provision (only on south side)

Wall pavement of thin slabs

Lower 40% of tower composed of large blocks hewn from local quarries

Exterior (north) face wall

Interior (south) face wall

Foundations up to 1.5 metres underground where bedrock permits

Fill of boulders and earth

Maximum width of Wall

Side view of a watchtower and cross-section of Wall adjoining it, typical of the Ming Dynasty (1368-1644) structures north of Beijing

them together. Bricks, some smaller, others larger than the common house bricks of today, were always bound together with mortar. The interior was filled with a mixture of rocks and earth. The top surface of the Wall, about five metres wide, was paved to a smooth surface with (usually) square slabs. On slopes of 45 degrees or more, the pavement was stepped.

Guards patrolling the Wall were protected from invaders by battlements, which averaged one and a half metres in height. They have small openings at pavement level for drainage. On the south side of the Wall waterspouts, usually carved from granite, were installed. Protruding by half a metre, they were never used on the north side, to prevent them making scaling the Wall easier. Loopholes and embrasures of various shapes existed for cannons and archers.

A special feature of the Ming Great Wall is its plethora of storeyed structures—watchtowers. Their classic design was pioneered by General Qi Jiguang, Governor General of Jizhou, one of the nine *zhen*, a military region corresponding to the present-day Hebei Province. In his treatise, *Records of Military Training*, the general advised the building of watchtowers wherever the Wall changed direction, on pinnacles, every 100 metres at key points and every 200-300 metres on gentle slopes. Several thousand watchtowers were built according to these

directions between Beijing and Shanhaiguan. They are wider than the Wall itself, protruding by up to five metres on the north side.

This design allowed archers in the tower to shoot from the flank at invaders scaling the Wall on ladders. For his work, Qi Jiguang was praised in *A History of the Ming Dynasty*, which chronicles the period: "Jizhou was the best administered and defended section of the Great Wall which no enemy was foolish enough to invade."

The most architecturally sophisticated buildings on the Great Wall were its gates and fortresses. The Jiayuguan fortress with its temple-like roofs, at the western terminus of the Ming Great Wall, probably boasts the finest examples of advanced gate and tower constructions.

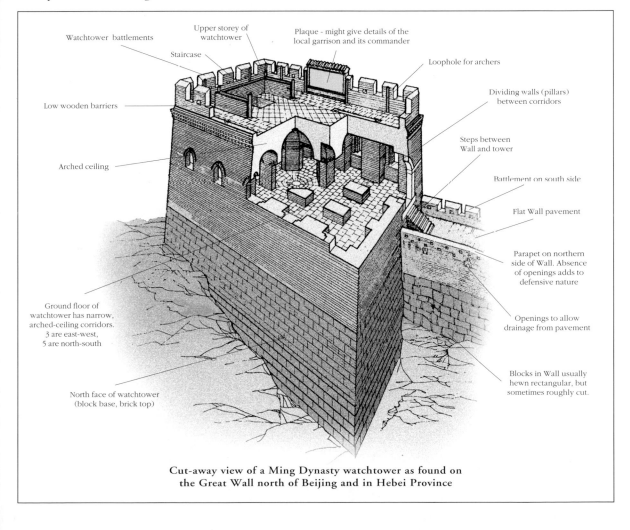

Watchtower battlements

Upper storey of watchtower

Plaque - might give details of the local garrison and its commander

Staircase

Loophole for archers

Low wooden barriers

Dividing walls (pillars) between corridors

Steps between Wall and tower

Arched ceiling

Battlement on south side

Flat Wall pavement

Parapet on northern side of Wall. Absence of openings adds to defensive nature

Ground floor of watchtower has narrow, arched-ceiling corridors. 3 are east-west, 5 are north-south

Openings to allow drainage from pavement

Blocks in Wall usually hewn rectangular, but sometimes roughly cut.

North face of watchtower (block base, brick top)

Cut-away view of a Ming Dynasty watchtower as found on the Great Wall north of Beijing and in Hebei Province

(Top) Rough blocks are bound by mortar. Here, on the outside (far) battlement, the bricks are stepped, while on the inside one, the bricks run parallel to the slope. (Bottom) A collapsed rampart affords a sectional view of the structure: brick sides and an earth/boulder fill.

But the Great Wall is not only a complex system of ramparts, towers and gates, it is also the story of the emperors and ministers who ordered its construction, of the generals and governors who recruited and administered the workforce and, above all, the heartbreaking story of tens of millions of men who built it with their bare hands, and who were left to guard it against invaders.

Life and Death—building, guarding and invading the Great Wall

Manpower for building the Great Wall through the centuries has come from the military, peasants and "convicts"—although most in the latter category had probably committed no crimes at all. According to Sima Qian's *Records of the Historian* (*c.* 100 BC), a 300,000-strong army, assisted by 500,000 peasants, laboured for approximately 12 years under General Meng Tian's direction to build the first Great Wall.

A legend from that time, that of Meng Jiangnu, tells of the heartbreak endured by those whose loved ones were conscripted into such labour. Meng Jiangnu lived in what is now Shaanxi Province, then the centre of the Qin empire, which had its capital in Xianyang, 30 kilometres northwest of Xi'an. Her husband was taken off to the border region. She travelled hundreds of kilometres one winter, to give him warm clothing, but was eventually told by other labourers that he had perished. Her grief was so intense that her tears flooded and washed away part of Qin Shihuangdi's Great Wall and revealed her husband's bones. On hearing that his defences had been damaged by the woman, the emperor summoned Meng Jiangnu to his palace for punishment. But, on seeing her beauty, Qin Shihuangdi

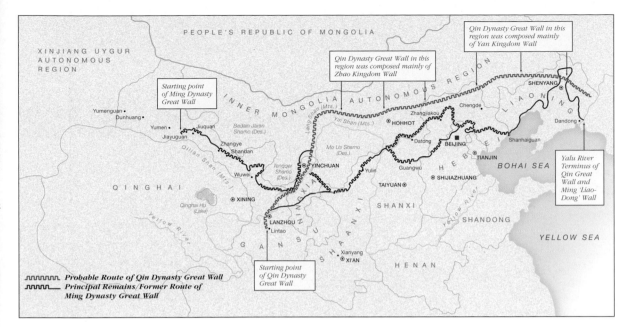

PEOPLE'S REPUBLIC OF MONGOLIA

XINJIANG UYGUR
AUTONOMOUS
REGION

Qin Dynasty Great Wall in this region was composed mainly of Yan Kingdom Wall

Qin Dynasty Great Wall in this region was composed mainly of Zhao Kingdom Wall

Starting point of Ming Dynasty Great Wall

INNER MONGOLIA AUTONOMOUS REGION

LIAONING

SHENYANG

Yumenguan •
Dunhuang •

Yumen •
Jiayuguan

Jiuquan

Badain Jaran Shamo (Des.)

Lang shan (Mts.)

Yin Shan (Mts.)

HOHHOT

Zhangjiakou

Chengde

Dandong •

Shanhaiguan

Zhangye
Shandan

Tengger Shamo (Des.)

Mo Us Shamo (Des.)

Datong

BEIJING

HEBEI

TIANJIN

Yalu River Terminus of Qin Great Wall and Ming 'Liao-Dong' Wall

QINGHAI

Wuwei

YINCHUAN

Yulin

Guangwu

SHIJIAZHUANG

BOHAI SEA

Qinghai Hu (Lake)

XINING

NINGXIA

TAIYUAN

SHANXI

Qilian Shan (Mts.)

LANZHOU
Lintao

GANSU

SHAANXI

SHANDONG

Yellow River

YELLOW SEA

Starting point of Qin Dynasty Great Wall

Xianyang
XI'AN

HENAN

꙳꙳꙳꙳꙳ **Probable Route of Qin Dynasty Great Wall**
꙳꙳꙳ **Principal Remains/Former Route of Ming Dynasty Great Wall**

wanted her as a concubine. Sickened by the thought, Meng Jiangnu fled and threw herself into the sea. A temple in Shanhaiguan, dating from at least the Northern Song period (960-1127), touchingly commemorates the heartbreak of Meng Jiangnu—and the millions of others whose family members died in slavery on the Great Wall.

Rulers of the Northern Dynasties, the Wei and Qi, used mainly peasant labour forces, on the pretext that the defence was aimed at stopping the advance of nomadic horsemen on the cultivated lands of China. Around 446 AD some 300,000 peasants were enlisted to build a rammed-earth Great Wall, to protect the Northern Wei capital of Pingcheng, now Datong in Shanxi Province. Similar numbers, several hundred thousand workers, but rarely more than a million, were used by Great Wall builders in other dynasties.

Worker numbers mushroomed during the Ming Dynasty, in order to cope with the vastly increased scale and extent of construction. Armies were enlarged and a new penal code established to ensure a constant supply of manpower for the work. Scores of offences were met with sentences of labour on the Great Wall. Even petty criminals were given life terms of work on the structure. More serious offenders received "perpetual" sentences. This meant that after the "convict" died working on the Great Wall, a member of his family—a son, brother, cousin or nephew—was sought as a replacement, inheriting the sentence. During the Ming Dynasty, censuses gave officials accurate information on the populace and family relationships, thus providing the administrative basis for operating such a draconian penal system.

(Below) An entrance archway to a watchtower.

Taking the backbreaking nature of the work into account, not to mention the searing heat and chilling cold of north China's summers and winters, it is unlikely that many labourers survived more than a year. The legend of Meng Jiangnu told that those who died constructing the Great Wall were immediately interred within the rock and earth fill of the structure, a belief that gave rise to the Great Wall being known as the world's longest cemetery. Folklore also told that the corpses actually bound the Wall together, while some believed that the mortar's white appearance came from crushed human bones. In the past this was regarded as a powerful ingredient of Chinese medicine in some rural areas adjacent to the Great Wall.

Imposing as the Great Wall appeared, its ultimate performance as a defence depended largely on the soldiers assigned to man it—their weapons, fighting ability and conviction when confronting invaders from the north.

During the Ming Dynasty, soldiers on this frontier wore armour of hide and wicker and were armed with bows and crossbows, to repel the enemy from up to 100 paces away. A variety of hand-held weapons—cudgels, axes, lances and halberds—were used for closer combat. Gunpowder, a Chinese invention dating back to the late 10th century, was used in cannon balls and smoke bombs. The latter distressed the horses on which the invaders relied.

Up to a score of men manned each watchtower but, despite their armoury, they could only thwart small attacks. Even the most strategic sections of the Wall, the passes, were garrisoned by relatively small units—up to a few thousand men. Instead of huge numbers of soldiers being stationed permanently on the Great Wall, the emperors and their ministers favoured swift communication of invasion and equally swift deployment of

(Preceding page) Despite building the strongest Great Wall in history, the Ming defences were breached on the coastal plain at Shanhaiguan. Manchu horsemen crossed the Wall here in 1644. (Top) Looking out from a watchtower, Gushanzi in Hebei. (Bottom) Locally available materials were always used — here in the desert that meant earth. The trench from which it was dug can be seen on the left, parallel to the Wall. This also accentuated the apparent height of the earthwork to the attacker.

(Top) The Great Wall is a familiar landmark to generations of peasants who have lived, and still live, in its shadow. A shepherd watches his flock north of the Wall in Yongchang County, Gansu.

reinforcements to counterattack.

Communication, smoke by day and fire by night, both supplemented by cannon fire, was effected by strings of beacons or smoking towers. They were situated both on and south of the Wall and some were within sight of the capital. A mixture of wolf dung, sulphur and potassium nitrate was used to make thick, black smoke.

According to military regulations issued in the reign of Chenghua (1465-1486), one fire and one salvo indicated an invasion force of 100 enemy soldiers; two fires and salvos indicated 500; three, 1,000; four, 5,000; five fires and salvos indicated 10,000 invaders. In good visibility and low winds, messages telling of invasion could probably have been sent 100 kilometres in less than one hour.

From the other, northern side of the Great Wall, the key invasion strategy was surprise. For much of its length the Wall was virtually insurmountable to any invader. Surprise attack, timed during bad weather, was vital because mountain mist and wind could obliterate signalling, both visually and audibly. Equipped with ladders, relatively small armies of tens of thousands of cavalry could threaten a dynasty if, for example, their attack was to coincide with internal strife that prevented the emperor's forces from counterattacking.

The most devastating invasion of the Great Wall was by the Mongols in

1211, when horsemen under Genghis Khan stormed across the Jin Dynasty defence of Inner Mongolia to take Juyongguan Pass, to the north of present day Beijing. Nevertheless, it was four more years before they took the Jin capital, Zhongdu, as that was protected by ten-metre-high city walls. Once in, they stayed for more than 150 years, until ousted by the founders of the Ming Dynasty.

Over four centuries later, the Manchus from the northeast faced an almost impregnable Ming Great Wall. They had tried unsuccessfully to breach the defence; finally, in 1644, a massive Manchu army was allowed to pass through the gates of Shanhaiguan by a renegade general at a time when the Ming Dynasty was already on the brink of ruin: Beijing had been seized by peasant rebels and Emperor Chongzhen had killed himself. The Manchus marched west and soon took Beijing. That not only spelt the end of the Ming Dynasty, but also an end to building and manning the Great Wall.

A new world order was dawning and enemies of the newly-established Qing Dynasty would come from across the globe, by sea from Europe, rather than the now empty wastes to the north of China. The main enemies of the Great Wall since 1644 have been natural—the advance of sand dunes in the west and rainfall, snow and earth tremors in the east. And time itself.

(Following pages) A magnificent watchtower and buttress on the interior Great Wall at Guangwu, north of Taiyuan, Shanxi. Over the years, local people have helped themselves to the blocks at the base of the tower and used them as building materials. (Page 32) Attracting more than 10,000 visitors per day, Badaling, reconstructed in the 1950s, is the most popular section of Wall for tourism. (Page 33) Old Dragon's Head on the Bohai coast at Shanhaiguan.